# Estate Sale Prospecting

# for Fun and Profit

## with *craigslist*® and *eBay*®

by
## JOHN LANDAHL

*an* **InfoStrategist.com** *book*

ISBN 1-59243-287-5

# Contents

# Summary

*craigslist* and *eBay* have created exciting new electronic venues for locating and reselling obscure but valuable estate sale items, making it easier to be a successful estate sale "prospector" today than ever before.

But with so many items to choose from at a typical estate sale, as well as other buyers to contend with, how can you quickly choose a few inexpensive items that you can resell at a significant profit, either as an interesting hobby or as an income-producing small business?

What will you need to plan for before you start? And how do you use *craigslist* and *eBay* to the greatest advantage? This book will help you get started!

*craigslist* is a registered trademark of craigslist, inc. *eBay* is a registered trademark of eBay Corp. *PayPal* is a registered trademark of *PayPal Corp*. "I Sold It" is a registered trademark of iSold It Corp. *Amazon.com* and *Amazon Marketplace* are registered trademarks of Amazon.com.

# *Antique Road Show* and You

Everyone has seen *Antique Road Show* episodes, where ordinary people are astounded to discover that a dusty and seemingly mundane lamp or dish they've recently discovered in their attic is actually a valuable but obscure antique worth thousands of dollars to the right collector! Do such items also turn up at estate sales, yard sales, and garage sales, sometimes for only a dollar or two? You bet they do, along with a great many more items of much lesser but still significant value!

But if you're not a knowledgeable, experienced antique dealer, how can you recognize them, and even if you could, how can you find that elusive collector to whom they have value? This book will give you some ideas for "prospecting" at estate sales (and garage sales, yard sales, and even in your own attic or basement) using the new tools provided *craigslist* and *eBay*.

# The Lessons of *Antique Road Show*

The radio airwaves (and probably your e-mail inbox as well!) are full of schemes and testimonials that promise ways to quickly make enormous amounts of money from home in your spare time using the Internet and your own computer. Often these schemes invoke the familiar name "*eBay*", although the fine print may mention that *eBay* itself is not by any stretch of the imagination a sponsor of them.

You don't have to watch *Antique Road Show* for long to realize that making lots of money quickly and easily is unlikely to happen in the field of estate sale prospecting, even bringing the magic name of *eBay* into the picture. Overlooked antiques and works of art worth thousands or tens of thousands of dollars are few and far between, and for items in these categories there are many pitfalls, including replicas, fakes, and frauds. It takes careful examination, sometimes with special techniques or equipment, as well as expert knowledge, to assess the value of an antique or work of art with any degree of assurance. On *Antique Road Show*, the resident antique expert will usually show display an impressive knowledge of obscure facts concerning the object presented for appraisal and point out subtle features or defects that increase or detract from its value.

Historical documents are particularly difficult to authenticate and may require expensive analysis of the composition of their paper and ink to establish the time period from which they date. Authors' and artists' signatures are all too susceptible to forgery.

Established antique dealers may be given early private access to estate sales or asked to appraise items of particular interest, but when the most enticing sales open to the public, they're frequently crowded and decisions on which items to purchase must often be made very quickly. This is especially true because the first customers in the door are often antique dealers and serious collectors who know exactly what they are looking for and will snap up valuable items they recognize, particularly jewelry and rare books.

As the popularity of *Antique Road Show* attests, in addition to dealers and collectors, there's no shortage of members of the general public who are also aware that antique items can be of considerable value, and no doubt many of the viewing audience make a point of going to estate sales (not to mention yard sales and garage sales) to look for them. Though they lack the expertise of dealers and serious collectors, amateurs will often immediately recognize certain widely-collected types of antiques, which they may snap up immediately. The excitement seen on *Antique Road Show* can definitely carry over to estate sales, and one hears stories of aggressively rude behavior, even to the point of someone snatching a particularly desirable item out of someone else's hand while they're looking at it!

When the estate sale includes collectibles, it's not uncommon to see one or two people familiar with the value of certain types of collectibles buying up quantities of a certain kind or sorting through sets to select the rarest and most valuable pieces. However, it's clear that among the widely-recognized items that disappear so quickly there are often also numerous obscure vintage items and collectibles of moderate value (say, $10 to $50) to a small collector.

These easily-overlooked items are typically "vintage" one-of-a-kind items, sometimes still in the original box, that have not been collected but simply squirreled away, and are often priced at between $1 and $10 at estate sales. You're not likely to see people fighting over these items at an estate sale because they're borderline "junk" as opposed to unmistakable antiques, and most people will be looking at them mainly to see if they are something they have a personal use for. Such borderline items are also generally not of sufficient value that establishing authenticity is a major issue, although there are certainly exceptions.

A quick glance at the catalog of a public library or the shelves of a major bookstore will confirm that there are a great many books available for those interested in antiques and collectibles. Today much of this information has now also been made conveniently available and searchable on the Internet.

There's also no shortage of books about selling on *eBay*, which is a complex subject about which a great deal can be said. This book is intended to supplement the information already available on this subject rather than to serve as a comprehensive guide.

# The New World of the Internet: *craigslist* and *eBay*

There's obviously nothing new about going to estate sales, buying items, and reselling them at a profit – antique dealers have been doing this for centuries. What *is* new is the ways the Internet provides for locating nearby estate sales (not to mention yard sales and garage sales!), for determining the value of items even if you're not an expert on them, and for reselling them into a national or even a global market. The two most important of these ways are *craigslist*, basically a huge, free electronic bulletin board, and *eBay*, which essentially creates a vast global electronic flea market.

## craigslist in Brief

In terms of the basic function it serves, *craigslist* is much like the classified ads section of the newspaper. However, unlike a newspaper, *craigslist* is free, electronically searchable, and has a very short lead time for publication of announcements. A new post will usually appear within about 15 minutes after submission.

Because it's free, estate sales will often be posted on *craigslist* as well as, or even instead of, in the newspaper classifieds. Taking advantage of the short lead time, estate sales will sometimes be posted on *craigslist* at the last moment.

*craigslist* has a local focus in the sense that it's easy to find postings within a particular metropolitan area. It also has a special category for garage sales in which estate sales are generally listed, making it especially easy to zero in on them.

## The *eBay* Behemoth

Unlike *craigslist*, *eBay* has a global rather than a local focus, making it easy to reach large numbers of potential buyers, and is an electronic auction system rather than an electronic bulletin board system. *eBay* is especially suitable for selling small, easy-to-ship items with reasonable assurance of getting the best possible price for them. Although, unlike *craigslist*, it charges modest fees to sellers, the advantages *eBay* provides far outweigh the cost for the kinds of items discussed here.

*eBay*'s key advantage is a way of substantially reducing the risk of online transactions to both buyers and sellers using a method called "public feedback," making large numbers of people comfortable with buying there. Other advantages include an enormous habitual user base, a well-thought-out and highly-detailed organization scheme making it easier for potential buyers to find a specific item, a convenient method of making secure electronic payments called *PayPal*, and various ways to make it easier for sellers to track sales and fill orders. A less-obvious but important feature made possible by

Internet technology is the use of color digital photographs so potential buyers have a clearer idea of what they are bidding on.

### The *My eBay* Page

Without going into detail here, an *eBay* member account includes a *My eBay* page with lists of items at auction and recently sold, making it easy to monitor auction progress, payments received, and items shipped.

## A Winning Combination

The combination of *craigslist* for quickly and easily locating nearby estate sales and *eBay* for selling small "vintage" items, particularly to collectors, at a sometimes-significant profit creates an exciting new opportunity for those interested in estate sale prospecting, either as an interesting and profitable hobby or as an income-producing small home-based business.

### Do You Have to Use *craigslist* and *eBay*?

Do you have to use *craigslist* and *eBay* for estate sale prospecting, or can you use other online bulletin boards and auction systems? Of course you can use other ways of finding estate sales, including the traditional method of looking for signs at street corners in your neighborhood, and of selling items online! *craigslist* and *eBay* are just the two most popular systems of these types. By all means use others if you find that they work well for you. For used books in particular, Amazon Marketplace may be the system of choice (see the Appendix).

# Is Estate Sale Prospecting for You?

Does estate sale prospecting, especially using *craigslist* and *eBay*, offer a real opportunity for enjoyment combined with the realization of significant income? Certainly, but it has its drawbacks as well, not the least of them the time commitment and meticulous attention to detail involved. The purpose of this book is not to convince or persuade you to take up estate sale prospecting, but rather to explore the subject in sufficient detail to enable you to make a well-informed decision as to whether the potential rewards are worth the effort.

If you do decide to try estate sale prospecting using *craigslist* and *eBay*, this book will give you a clear idea of how to get started, the things you need to plan for, the frustrations and obstacles you are likely to encounter, and some suggestions for overcoming them. Some things I say here may strike you as nothing more than common sense ("pack fragile items carefully for shipping"). However, estate sale prospecting is a complex enough activity that a thorough summary is useful.

## A Quick Test

If you just want to try out estate sale prospecting to see what its potential is and live near an "I Sold It On *eBay*" store, you can try going to an estate sale or two and buying a few items that you think will sell for $30 or more apiece on *eBay*. Then take them to the "I Sold It On *eBay*" store, open an account, and they will photograph, list, sell, and ship the items for you.

You'll receive at least 60% of the price after fees if an item sells (more for more expensive items) and pay nothing if it does not. Within two weeks you'll find out if your items sell profitably or not, without needing your own *eBay* account, digital camera, packing materials, and so forth. You'll find more about this option in the next section.

# Before You Begin

Before you make the decision to embark on estate sale prospecting using *craigslist* and *eBay*, you should give careful consideration to your specific situation. This includes where you live and your personal strengths.

Estate sale prospecting will be most successful in established urban areas because nearby estate sales with a high proportion of vintage items will occur more frequently. If you live on an isolated cattle ranch in Nevada, I speak from experience in saying that you will not find two or three estate sales within reasonable driving distance coming up every weekend!

Your geographic location is by no means the only factor to consider. To sell successfully long-term on *eBay*, you'll need certain personal qualities, including patience, persistence, meticulous attention to detail, a capacity for follow-through, and a tolerance for pressure and tedium.

If your personality doesn't match up well against these requirements, you definitely don't want to embark on estate sale prospecting as a solo venture! Instead, think about teaming up with someone else, perhaps a spouse or a buddy, with whom you can share those tasks that are not your forte.

You should read carefully through the next section, "What You'll Need To Get Started," to be sure that you already have or will be able to obtain everything you'll need to pursue estate sale prospecting.

## An Urban Option

If you live in a major metropolitan area, you can also investigate the "I Sold It On *eBay*" stores that handle (for a fee, naturally!) all the myriad details involved with *eBay* sales and will keep you from having to worry about things like item descriptions, digital photographs, postal scales, and packing materials. However, keep in mind that these stores accept only items that can be expected to sell for more than a certain dollar value ($30 at the time of this writing) with a minimum starting bid of $9.99.

The types of items described here may not have a value that can easily be established, so they may not be readily accepted by an "I Sold It On *eBay*" store. Fortunately you can find out in advance by searching yourself for similar items on *eBay* before taking them to an "I Sold It On *eBay*" store.

# What You'll Need to Get Started

To get started in estate sale prospecting using *craigslist* and *eBay*, you'll need a computer equipped with a Web browser, a broadband Internet connection, an *eBay* account, a digital camera you can connect to your computer, a method of transportation, some cash, a postal scale, and some packaging materials, including sturdy cardboard boxes, cushioning, and strong tape. You'll also need a little storage space and some spare time, probably more than you would think at first! And although you can get by without one, I strongly recommended opening a *PayPal* account if you don't already have one.

## Key Advantages of *PayPal*

*PayPal*, although only covered briefly in this book, it's an important adjunct to estate sale prospecting because it provides a fast, secure, convenient, and widely-used electronic payment method combined with some useful features specifically designed for *eBay* auctions.

## The Computer and Web Browser

Almost any computer manufactured in the last five years will do, as long as it can connect to the Internet and has a Web browser like Firefox, Microsoft Internet

Explorer, or Apple Safari, as well as a USB port for connecting a digital camera or a card reader to upload pictures of items to sell.

## The Internet Connection

A broadband Internet connection of some sort is important, otherwise using *eBay*, especially uploading digital photos, will be painfully slow. However, it's not important whether the connection is DSL, cable, or wi-fi, and it need not be a premium-priced service.

## The *eBay* Account

You'll need to sign up for an *eBay* account if you don't already have one. There's no registration fee, but to obtain a seller's account you'll need to provide a credit card number because *eBay* charges modest fees for posting and selling items.

If you're just curious to learn more, you can sign into *eBay* as a guest and view items that are for sale. However, you must have an account to view completed sales and see what items actually sold for, as well as which items did not sell. This is definitely useful information to have when putting items up for auction!

## The Digital Camera

An important part of selling an item on *eBay*, especially a one-of-a-kind collectible item where condition is important, is to add at least one color digital photograph of it to the listing. While items can be listed without a photograph, this is generally not advisable. Ideally the photograph should be clear as opposed to blurred or fuzzy and should show the item close-up so that details like stains or nicks are visible. However, the basic *eBay* photo size is 400 x 400 pixels, or only 0.16 megapixels, so an inexpensive digital camera will suffice for most purposes, especially since it will probably only be necessary to take a dozen or so pictures at a time.

If you don't have a suitable camera already, you may be able to find one on *craigslist* for $70 or less. The main thing you'll need to look for in a camera is a way to upload pictures to your computer. Most digital cameras have a USB port for this purpose. Another method is to eject the memory card or stick from the camera and insert it into a card reader connected to your computer to upload pictures.

One challenge you're likely to encounter is taking clear, detailed close-ups of small items. For this purpose it helps to have a camera that can be mounted on a tripod. Also helpful is a self-timer feature to minimize camera motion during the exposure.

A macro photo mode is designed for taking close-ups. If your camera has no macro mode but does have an optical zoom, setting it up further back from the item and then zooming in on it can improve clarity of the image. If the camera has sufficient resolution (say, 2 or 3 megapixels), it may also work to take a photograph from several feet away and then crop and enlarge the item using standard image processing software, which can also be used to adjust color and brighten dark images.

**A Note on Image Processing Software**

*Adobe PhotoShop* is probably the most commonly used program for editing digital images. However, a number of less expensive programs, including those supplied with digital cameras or with computer operating systems, will provide the minimal features needed to crop images and adjust color levels for selling on *eBay*.

## The Transportation

The main thing to keep in mind here is that if you find items you want to buy at estate, garage, or yard sales, you'll need to bring them back home afterwards. Bicycling, for example, may be a convenient and enjoyable way to get to an estate sale and will avoid parking problems, but will it also be a convenient way to get a load of possibly heavy, bulky items home undamaged? I've certainly seen satisfied shoppers at estate sales who came by bicycle – you just need to keep the return trip in mind. The same goes for traveling by bus.

If you have a car, driving may be the obvious choice for transportation, but keep in mind that the cost of gas is an expense – not a big issue if you're pursuing estate sale prospecting as a hobby, but more important if you're doing it as a business activity. Of course, you may be able to team up with a friend who also enjoys going to estate sales and share driving expenses.

## The Cash

Sellers at estate, garage, and yard sales will seldom accept checks or credit cards, so plan to take enough cash to buy several items. This need not be a great deal, especially at first, since you'll be looking for obscure vintage items masquerading as junk rather than the widely-recognized collectibles with their higher price tags. $10 to $20 may be sufficient on many days.

## The Postal Scale

You'll need a way to weigh items before listing them on *eBay* so prospective buyers can factor shipping costs into their bidding decisions. And you need to be able to obtain accurate shipping weights, otherwise you may underestimate how much to charge for shipping and consequently undercharge for this service. You may also want to use *PayPal* to purchase and print out you own shipping labels to avoid having to stand in line at the counter at the post office, in which case you'll definitely need to weigh parcels accurately so they're not returned to you for insufficient postage.

Chances are you'll need to be able to weigh items ranging from an ounce or two (for example, a baseball trading card) to 5 lbs. or more (like a heavy vase in a sturdy box). However, if you think you'll also be buying and reselling items like framed pictures or power tools, you'll need a scale with greater capacity.

Postal scales are sold by the U.S. Postal Service at post offices as well as by office supply stores. Electronic postal scales with digital readouts are priced according to weight capacity, and range in price from $30 to over $100.

## A Make-Do Alternative

Don't want to spend a lot of money for a postal scale, especially a high-capacity one? If you're willing to put up with a little inconvenience, you may find you can get by with a $20 hand-held digital fishing scale like the ones sold in the sporting goods sections of larger chain stores.

You'll need to put each item you want to weigh in a large plastic bag you can hang from the hook on the scale in order to weigh it. You'll also want to check the accuracy of your fishing scale against a post office scale.

To be sure that you purchase sufficient postage, *always add one ounce* to the weight reported by the fishing scale. This will cost you a little in unnecessary postage on an occasional item, but will avoid the inconvenience and lengthy shipping delays if packages are returned to you for insufficient postage.

## The Shipping Materials

You'll need a variety of packaging materials, including sturdy cardboard boxes of various sizes, cushioning material, and strong tape. If you're like most *eBay* sellers, you'll probably be able to make do by recycling boxes and packing materials; you may already have some set aside. Crumpled newspaper, chintzy though it may be, is often adequate for cushioning.

Unless you decide that it's just more convenient to buy boxes, envelopes, and cushioning material, your only out-of-pocket expense here will be for packaging tape, which does need to be strong, but not necessarily a major brand. Stores like Target often carry their own inexpensive brand. You'll find that *eBay* buyers are not offended to receive oddly-wrapped parcels provided the contents are undamaged.

## The Storage Space

The key thing about storage space is to have enough room to organize your (possibly numerous!) items as you acquire them, photograph them, list them, pack them, and ship them. Obviously you don't want to misplace any items and not be able to find them when it comes time to ship them.

Neither do you want to ship a buyer the wrong item by accident! Even something as simple as a cabinet with several shelves can help you keep your items organized.

## The Spare Time

Estate sale prospecting is simple in concept, but you may find the actual activities involved surprisingly, even discouragingly, time-consuming to complete. Several of these activities basically fall into that frustrating category where the best way to figure out the time needed is to estimate how long they will take, then multiply by 3!

If you pursue estate sale prospecting as a hobby, you'll probably find many of the tasks involved pleasant and undemanding, and therefore regard them as part of an enjoyable pastime that happens to bring in a little money. If, however, you are pursuing estate sale prospecting as a business opportunity, it's important not to underestimate the time demands, which will be discussed in detail in the section "Where Does All the Time Go" below. At this point, suffice it to say that reviewing descriptions of similar items that have sold recently on *eBay* is one example of an activity which can be both interesting and time-consuming; another is responding to questions from bidders.

## The *PayPal* Account

Although the *PayPal* online payment service is owned by *eBay*, it requires a separate account, which is optional in the sense that you can sell on *eBay* without one by accepting payment in the form of checks and money orders. However, a *PayPal* account provides several important advantages that more traditional payment methods do not.

At the heart of *PayPal* is a fast, secure, convenient, and widely-used electronic payment system. This system has been tailored to speed *eBay* auction transactions by linking to the *eBay* system. *PayPal* also provides several convenience features for auctions, including confirmed mailing addresses for buyers to eliminate shipping errors and an easy way to issue refunds if the need arises.

All this comes at a price, since *PayPal* does charge sellers transaction fees which are automatically deducted from payments as they are received. However, *PayPal* also provides some valuable services, such as the ability to print shipping labels and seller protection for shipments, at no cost. In addition, U.S. Postal Service Delivery Confirmation is free for Priority Mail when printing your own shipping labels, saving a little money for a commonly-used shipping method. *PayPal* also pays interest on account balances, compensating to some degree for its transaction fees in yet another way.

# The Basic Process Step by Step

The basic estate sale prospecting process is straightforward enough, but it does involve a number of steps. You locate a nearby estate sale, go to it, identify a few inexpensive but promising items, buy them, take them home, photograph them, write brief descriptions of them, determine their shipping weights, find the appropriate listing categories, set the starting bid amounts, and list them on *eBay*. You answer e-mail questions about them from prospective buyers and ship those that sell, ideally at a pleasing profit, and receive good feedback, bolstering your reputation as an reliable *eBay* seller and leaving feedback for your buyers in return.

This process can be divided into four major sections – finding items, selling items, shipping items, and wrap-up.

## Finding Estate Sales

As discussed earlier, to find nearby estate sales (and garage and yard sales), searching *craigslist* for your local area will almost certainly be your quickest and most convenient method, although of course newspaper classified ads are an option too. Because posting ads on *craigslist* is free and has an extremely short lead time, some sales may be posted there that will not appear in the classifieds.

Start by using your Web browser to go to the URL *http://www.craigslist.com*. On the main *craigslist* web page, find your state and from there your local area. Next, click on the *"Garage Sales"* category within the *"For Sale"* section. Estate and yard sales as well as garage sales are almost invariably listed here. In the search box put in *"estate sale"* and click *"Search"* to narrow the list for easier examination. Keep in mind that estate sales may be posted only a day or two in advance.

It may be helpful to use an Internet mapping program like MapQuest or Google Maps to pinpoint the location of a sale if it's in an unfamiliar neighborhood.

### The Mislabeled Sale

There's no official definition for "estate sale," so once in awhile you may encounter a sale billed as an estate sale which you would consider more of a garage or yard sale in terms of the types of items offered. Conversely, you may occasionally run across a sale modestly billed as a "yard sale," but with many estate-sale type items. You may be able to get a good idea from a *craigslist* posting what types of items you will find a a particular sale.

## Selecting Items to Purchase

Selecting the right items to purchase is obviously the tricky part, especially when you have to make snap decisions as one of a crowd of eager buyers at the beginning of a sale. It usually will not make sense to buy a large number of items, for several reasons.

First, each item will take a fair amount of time to sell on *eBay*. Second, you can only carry so much at one time as you shop at an estate sale, although if you bring a bag or basket, you can select more items with less risk of dropping or crushing some of them. Third, each item represents an investment of money which may or may not be recouped later on, so the more items you buy, the more money you risk.

Keep in mind that even if you see an item that you think is particularly valuable, you may later discover that you are wrong, for example, because it turns out to be a reproduction rather than an original. Markets can also change in a short time, occasionally dramatically.

Ideally you'd like to be able to zero in on two or three items per sale that have a good likelihood of being worthwhile to resell. For starters, look for items that appear to date from 1970 or earlier, are in good condition, and are still in their original boxes. Hand tools are one example; items of home decor are another. Books and items of jewelry are trickier.

Selecting the right items is obviously the key to successful estate sale prospecting, so this topic will be discussed in greater depth later on.

## Selling Items on *eBay*

The numerous steps involved with listing and selling items on *eBay* are described in detail in the next chapter.

# Selling Items on *eBay*

Listing and selling items on *eBay* is a complex process that involves searching for similar items, choosing a listing category, writing a title, uploading a digital photograph, writing a brief description, setting a starting price, entering the shipping weight, setting the shipping methods, setting the return policy, reviewing the listing, and posting it. Attention to detail is important here, but fortunately you'll also be able to revise your listing as much as you need to until the first bid is placed.

And you'll be able to resume work on a listing if you are interrupted before you finish it for some reason. As the auction progresses, you may receive questions about your item from potential bidders, giving you the opportunity to add more information.

It's definitely a good idea to begin your bookkeeping process at this point by recording the amount you paid for each item you just purchased in a spreadsheet. If you pursue estate sale prospecting actively and purchase a number of items over a period of weeks, you may find that by the time their sale at auction is completed, you've forgotten exactly how much you paid for a particular one.

# Reviewing Similar Listings

Use any information you have about an item, such as a product name, a manufacturer, or a model number, to search *eBay* for similar items as though you were looking for one to buy. This initial step can be time-consuming, but it will give you valuable information about the most popular categories for listing items of this particular nature, what to be sure to mention in the item title and description, what starting bids other sellers have set, and how active a market exists for items like this.

If you log into your *eBay* account, you'll also be able to search completed sales, not just active listings, so you'll be able to see what items like yours have been selling for recently, which can also help you set your starting bid. The listing for a similar item that's brought a high price can be particularly useful because it provides an example of how to write a good title and description.

# Choosing a Listing Category

For collectible items, the best listing category to choose is the one with the largest number of similar items because that's the category that collectors are most likely to browse. You can also list an item in multiple categories, but that entails additional expense and may not give any better results than a well-chosen single category.

When you begin to create a listing, *eBay* provides a way to see which categories are most commonly used to list similar items. This will be most useful if you've already decided on a good title for your item (see next section). Reviewing listings for similar items in the first step described above will also help you determine which category to choose.

## The Title

The item title is critical because it's what most potential bidders will use to zero in on items of particular interest to them. The title is brief, so it needs to be carefully worded to convey the most important aspects to buyers. It should be as specific as possible – "Unused Vintage Small Glass Kerosene Lamp" as opposed to "Lovely Lamp!"

If you're fortunate, you may be able to find one or two listings for very similar, perhaps even identical, items that sold for an unusually high price and see how their titles are worded. Be sure important words in the title are spelled correctly, otherwise your listing may be missed by collectors searching *eBay* for a specific item.

## The Photograph

A color photograph is essential when you sell an item on *eBay* because it gives a potential buyer a quick way of confirming what an item is and assessing its quality. However, for many items an amateur snapshot-quality photograph will be perfectly adequate, so it's unnecessary to spend a lot of time getting a magazine-quality photograph.

Regardless of the original size of the photograph you upload, the eBay system will automatically shrink it to 400 pixels by 400 pixels, so you'll probably want to use image-processing software like Adobe PhotoShop on your computer to crop your photographs so they fill most of the frame. Depending on the characteristics of your digital camera, you may also want to adjust the color levels of the photo so it looks more like the actual item. Save your photograph with a meaningful name so you can easily identify it when it is time to upload it to *eBay*.

For an additional fee, you can add more photographs to your listing. However, for many items a single photograph is sufficient. This is particularly true for vintage collectible items the value of which is unknown to you. If an item turns out to be particularly valuable, bidders may e-mail you with a request to post additional photographs.

## The Description

The item description can be brief, but should be accurate and include a description of any defects or flaws. Reviewing the descriptions of similar items which have brought a good price can be very helpful in deciding what to include and important characteristics to mention.

## The Listing Duration

How long should your item be listed at auction? *eBay*'s default setting of 7 days is a good starting point. There may be reasons for choosing a shorter or longer duration for a particular item, but that's beyond the scope of this book. You'll find this topic discussed in detail in books on selling on *eBay* and in *eBay*'s online guides.

## The Starting Bid

What amount should you choose in setting the starting bid? If you look over item listings, you'll see starting bids on *eBay* as low as $0.99 even for items that eventually sell for hundreds of dollars. Occasionally you'll even see a starting bid as low as $0.01, giving the message that someone just wants to find another home for an item, unless, as sometimes happens, their idea is to make money on shipping and handling.

The listing insertion fee for selling an item on *eBay* is based on the amount of the starting bid, so setting a low starting bid will save you money on fees. On the other hand, a low starting bid can give potential buyers a message that you believe the item to be of little value. If you know that an item is valuable, you can set a high enough starting bid to ensure that if it sells, you'll make a profit. Another way to ensure this is by setting a reserve on an item, but a high reserve on something with a low starting bid usually comes as an unpleasant surprise to early bidders and may alienate potential buyers, reducing the competition for your item.

Do items with low starting bids ultimately sell for less than similar ones with higher starting bids? It's by no means clear that this is the case, especially for collectible items. If it were, that would create an opportunity for people to buy items listed with low starting bids on *eBay*, then resell them with higher starting bids, assuming that the difference in final price exceeds shipping costs. Nonetheless, it makes sense to review recently completed sales of items similar to your to see how other sellers set their starting bids.

## The Shipping Weight

You'll want to know the shipping weight of the item, or at least have a good estimate of it, before you post your listing so prospective bidders will know what their overall cost for the item will be. The most accurate way to determine the shipping weight is to pack the item in its box or envelope so it's ready to ship, then weigh it.

However, since you don't know if the item will sell or not, you may not wish to take the time to pack it at this point, so you may want to use an estimated shipping weight instead. One way to estimate the shipping weight is to put the item in the box or envelope in which you intend to ship it, along with a generous amount of packing material, weigh the box, and add a few ounces to compensate for the tape and shipping label you'll add later. This is also a good time to measure your item if it's one for which listings of similar items indicate that dimensions are important.

## Choosing the Shipping Methods

*eBay* makes it possible to offer a range of shipping options to successful bidders, for example, U.S. Postal Service Priority Mail as well as Parcel Post. U.S. Postal Service Priority Mail is a popular option for small collectible items, especially ones that will fit in a flat rate box or envelope.

If you use *PayPal* to print your own shipping labels, you can simply give parcels to your letter carrier, saving yourself a trip to the post office and time waiting in line at the counter. Some post offices have automated 24-hour postal centers where you can weigh envelopes and packages and buy postage with a credit or debit card, often without having to wait in line at all.

Media Mail is the obvious choice for books, videotapes, DVDs, and audio books. For large items, you may want to offer UPS shipping methods, especially if you live near a UPS location. FedEx is certainly another possibility.

When you select the shipping methods to offer, you also have the option to add a handling charge at this point. Whether you choose to do so and, if so, how much you will charge, is entirely up to you. If you look over a few *eBay* listings, you'll see that handling charges vary enormously. Some sellers don't charge at all for handling, while others may charge anywhere from $2 to $10 per item.

There's no question that some buyers object strongly to handling charges they consider exorbitant. However, most buyers probably simply factor in the shipping and handling in deciding how much they'll bid for an item, so a higher handling charge will simply result in a lower sale price.

## Your Return Policy

Your return policy for *eBay* items is also up to you. If you review *eBay* listings, you'll see that some items are sold "as-is, no returns."

I personally offer a 14-day, "complete satisfaction guaranteed" return policy on most items, since I'd rather take a loss on an item that receive negative feedback from a dissatisfied buyer. I've seldom had anyone take me up on this, and, so thus far I've seen no reason to shift to a more restrictive return policy. However, keep in mind that vintage cameras and electronic equipment like phonograph turntables that you find at estate sales may not be in good working order and will have a higher likelihood of being returned as defective than other types of items. If you don't intend to accept a item back regardless of any defects the buyer may report, be sure to indicate clearly in the listing that it's being sold "as is."

### PayPal Makes Refunds Easy

If you need to issue a refund for an item purchased using PayPal, go to the transaction details and look near the bottom for a "Refund Payment" link. PayPal will refund the full payment amount to the buyer and you will pay no fees at all for the transaction.

## Reviewing the Listing

The final step in posting an *eBay* listing is to review it. At this step you'll also see a breakdown of the fees associated with the listing.

Obviously it makes sense to review the entire listing at this stage, paying special attention to the title, photograph, and item description. However, rest assured that if you realize that you need to make changes after you submit the listing, you'll be able to do so right up until the first bid is placed.

### Stick with the Basics

The *eBay* system will helpfully suggest various ways to improve your listing at this point, most of them at additional cost. As discussed later on, start off with the most basic possible listings, then experiment with extra features as you gain experience to see if they make a difference or not when auctioning vintage collectible items.

## Questions from Bidders

*eBay* includes its own e-mail system called "My Messages" which allows bidders to send questions to sellers in a way that blocks out most e-mail spam and scams. In fact, if you receive an e-mail that appears to come from or through *eBay* but doesn't appear in your "My Messages" inbox, it's without doubt a scam of some sort.

## Beware this *PayPal* E-mail Scam!

Watch out for this particularly deceptive *PayPal* "phishing" scam! It's an official-looking e-mail with "Security Center Alert!" or "Please Restore Your Account Access" in the subject line that purports to notify you of suspicious *PayPal* account activity. The e-mail goes on to inform you that access to your *PayPal* account has been limited and will be suspended if you don't click on a link at the bottom and update your information.

DON'T DO IT! The usual advice NEVER to click on a link in an e-mail and enter financial information DEFINITELY applies here!

Instead, forward the e-mail to *PayPal*'s spoof@paypal.com mailbox so they're aware of it, then go to http://www.paypal.com and log directly into your account in the usual way. Rest assured that if there are indeed any issues with your *PayPal* account, you'll be informed of them on the first screen you see, and that when you check your account you'll find that your access to it has not been limited in any way.

This is by no means the only highly official-looking e-mail scam that may come your way! ANY e-mail that threatens to suspend your *PayPal* account is highly suspicious, no matter how convincing it appears, especially if it gives an alarmingly short period to "verify your personal informaton" like 72 hours. The best thing to do if you think an e-mail is actually from *PayPal* and your account is really going to be suspended is to call their customer service number, 1-888-221-1161, to check. They'll be able to tell you if the e-mail you received is genuine or not.

You can expect to receive legitimate e-mail questions about vintage collectible items, especially valuable ones, and it's a good practice to check daily for such messages and respond promptly to them. If you respond through *eBay*'s "My Messages," you'll have the option of posting the question and your response at the bottom of your item description. This can save you time in responding to similar questions and will also indicate to bidders that there's interest in your item.

## Monitoring Auction Progress

Once your listing's been posted, the auction itself will basically run on autopilot without any intervention on your part, and when it concludes *eBay* will send you an e-mail telling you whether your item sold or not, and if so, for how much. However, it's natural to want see whether any bids have been placed on your item as the auction progresses, and *eBay* provides a list of items you're selling on its "My eBay" page, along with summary information including the auction end date, the number of bids, the high bid amount, and the number of "watchers" (see below). It will usually take several days before an item starts to draw bids, and sometimes most of the action occurs in the last few minutes when experienced bidders jump in after holding back earlier to avoid betraying their interest.

However, even if an item doesn't draw bids at first, it may draw "watchers," prospective bidders whose attention has been caught by the item but are waiting to see how the bidding goes before making a decision to bid themselves. The number of watchers is shown only to the seller, not to other buyers, and it can be quite interesting to keep an eye on as the auction progresses.

However, keep in mind that people may watch an item for various reasons other than wanting to buy it. For example, they may be planning to sell a similar one soon and want to see how well yours does. For this reason, a large number of watchers doesn't automatically translate into a bidding war for an item when it closes.

## Shipping Items

Shipping items is relatively straightforward, especially if you're receiving auction payments and printing your own shipping labels using *PayPal*. One key thing is to package each item well enough to keep it from being damaged, for example, in a corrugated cardboard box surrounded by packing material.

Another is to use a large enough box or envelope to attach the shipping label without folding it around the package. This will usually require a box or envelope at least 8" high and 6" wide.

The shipping label should be firmly attached to the package, especially around the edges, so it will not be ripped off during postal handling. However, tape shouldn't be placed over the barcodes, otherwise they may not scan properly.

If you live in an apartment building or an urban area, you may want to take packages containing valuable items directly to the post office or personally hand them to the letter carrier to ensure that they're not stolen before they're picked up.

## Leaving Feedback

It may at first seem like unnecessary extra work, but you'll find that leaving feedback for buyers is an important part of successful selling long-term on *eBay*. The best time to do this will usually be after a buyer has received their item and left feedback, hopefully positive, for you. Leaving feedback, ideally positive as well, returns the courtesy and helps buyers establish or maintain their status as reputable *eBay* members.

### Avoid Leaving Negative Feedback

If you're just starting out on *eBay*, a good idea is NEVER to leave negative feedback for ANYONE until you have at least 20 transactions to your credit. The reason for this is that if you leave negative feedback for someone, they'll probably leave negative feedback for you in return. If you have fewer than 20 transactions and one negative feedback comment, your overall feedback rating will be less than 95%, which may discourage some prospective bidders.

## Final Accounting

Once you've received payment for your item and paid the shipping costs, you're in a position to tally up the acquisition cost, the *eBay* and *PayPal* fees, together with any other expenses of making the sale, so you can see if you're operating profitably or not. Obviously profitability is a more important consideration if you're approaching estate sale prospecting as a business venture than if you regard it primarily as a hobby. If you offer a return policy, you may occasionally find you have to refund money for a defective item. If you're operating as a business, you'll probably already know that customer returns, disappointing as they may be, are considered a normal cost of doing business.

### Remember the *My eBay* Page

Your *My eBay* page has a link called "Seller Account" that gives you convenient access to billing details, including all the fees associated with listing and selling a particular item.

# Some Remarkable Finds!

What sorts of easily-overlooked items might one find for under $10 at an estate sale that could turn out to have much greater value at auction on *eBay*? As a starting point, items most people frequenting estate sales would remember as commonplace from their own childhoods. Here are some examples of items I've turned up and profited from in my own estate sale prospecting.

Keep in mind that what's important about the items described here is their shared characteristics, like being in their original box so that you have the name of the item as well as that of its manufacturer. There will be little point in keeping an eye out for more of these particular items at estate sales because they're quite rare; they're just examples of types of things to experiment with buying and reselling.

## An Old Box of Marbles

This item is the one that got me interested in estate sale prospecting to begin with, though it actually came from a musty closet, not an estate sale! My former spouse had asked for my help in cleaning out her closets and sorting through years of accumulated belongings. Some we kept, others we set aside to take to a nearby consignment store, yet others we saved to donate to a thrift store, and what was left went into the garbage.

When we got to an old cardboard box of marbles about half and inch thick and four inches square, my first reaction was to toss it in the garbage bag because, much as I had enjoyed playing marbles as a boy, I knew that kids seldom do any more, and I assumed old marbles would have no value even for a thrift store. However, Nancy sensibly asked if it might not be a better idea to try selling them on *eBay* first and I agreed. When I checked *eBay* later on, I was surprised to find that there was indeed an active market for old marbles.

The box was labeled "AKRO AGATE COMPANY" with the slogan "STRAIGHT AS A KRO FLIES," a reference to the quality of the marbles it contained. The assortment of marbles inside it included "clearies" and cats-eyes, reminding me of the ones I had prized so much as a child, when I placed second one year in my small town's annual marble tournament. I also enjoyed finding about a little about the company, which turned out to have patented a mechanical method for manufacturing glass marbles in 1915 and to have gone out of business in 1951 after branching out into manufacturing other types of glass items as well.

This item was interesting enough to collectors that questions were raised about its authenticity soon after I listed it on *eBay*. We had difficulty answering because them authoritatively had been given to us by my Nancy's father several years before. Although we assumed it was a memento from his childhood, we couldn't be absolutely certain about that. Seeking to assess the authenticity, one potential bidder e-mailed me with a request for additional photographs of the box. Had we been in a different part of the country, we might have been able to have the marbles appraised by a professional marble grader, but that wasn't an option where we lived. Nonetheless, the box went for $94 at auction on *eBay* and after receiving them the winning bidder left feedback saying "gorgeous item!"

This experience led me to start searching out estate sales and to look at the items offered there with different eyes.

# A 1950's Japanese Glass Wind Chime

When I first saw the faded, flimsy box with its illustration of a small 1950's Japanese wind chime early on the first day of a small neighborhood estate sale, my reaction was that this item was unlikely to have any value at all. However, the estate sale managers had recognized it as a vintage item and priced it at $3, unlike the $0.50 items around it on the same shelf. I dimly remembered Japanese glass wind chimes like this from my own childhood as being cheap and fragile, but I bought it anyway.

When I got it home and looked at it more closely, I found it was so delicate that I didn't even want to take the risk of removing it from its packing material when I photographed it for *eBay* – I just pulled the excelsior back a little to see that the wind chime was there and still intact. To my surprise, when I posted it on *eBay* it soon attracted considerable interest and eventually sold for $40 to someone in Virginia who was delighted to get it and wrote in her feedback, "I love my item, thank you very much!"

# A 1960's Yankee Hand Drill

At the same sale, I found a 1960's Yankee hand drill in the basement, still in its original box. Again, the estate sale managers had recognized it as a vintage item and priced it at $8. I appreciated this item a little more than the wind chime because I remembered once owning a similar one and took a chance on it too.

When I checked *eBay* after buying it, I found that there was a surprisingly good market for drills like this, and that one in good condition, as this one was, could be expected to sell for between $20 and $30. This particular one turned out to be especially desirable and went for $52 to someone in Minnesota!

## Truly a National, Even a Global, Market!

I've shipped items to buyers in almost every state as well as to Canada and Great Britain. Obviously posting items on *eBay* allows a seller to tap into a much broader market than can be found in any one city or neighborhood, however extensive or densely populated!

# Mistakes I've Made

"How-to" books like this one typically emphasize examples of successes, which are always interesting, useful, and motivating, and I've described a couple of highly profitable purchases in the preceding section. However, in this book I'll also give some examples of unprofitable selections, which can be equally instructive.

Mistakes I've made include overestimating the antiquity of an item, overestimating the market for a item, and yielding to the temptation to buy an unsuitable item. Many of the mistakes I've made haven't cost me much money, but a few fall into the more disheartening category of expensive lessons.

## Overestimating Antiquity

At one estate sale I saw an attractive wooden boxed set of heart keepsake jewelry, opened but apparently unused, for $5. Many other items at the sale dated from the 1950's or 1960's, and I assumed that this was also a "vintage" item. The sale was just starting and I didn't take the time to examine the cover closely, so I missed the date that was in fine print at the bottom – 2005! Not vintage at all!

When I checked *eBay* later on, I found that I wasn't the only one to be misled about this item – another seller had listed the same set in the "vintage jewelry" category. Their listing had gotten no bids, perhaps because knowledgeable buyers had recognized it as contemporary and probably thought the seller was trying to scam them.

I listed it in a more appropriate category, but didn't get any bids either! Since then I've looked a little more closely at items and avoided contemporary jewelry! Fortunately I was able to recover my initial investment on this particular item by selling it later at a yard sale, where buyers could pick it up and look at it.

## Overestimating the Market

On the final day of an estate sale I impulsively bought an antique-looking Durham Duplex straight razor for $5 from the jewelry table, attracted to it because of its elegant ivory-colored handle. At least I didn't pay the marked price of $10 for it, as I would have on the first day of the sale!

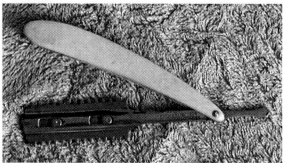

When I checked *eBay* later in the day I was disappointed to find several of these razors for sale, but none had actually sold within the past couple of months. I was utterly mistaken in thinking that there would be a market for this item just because I was drawn to it!

## Yielding to Temptation

At one suburban estate sale, I made the mistake of purchasing a very heavy item I had no idea how to describe – a 18" tall cement garden sculpture of a seated Hindu deity for $5. This statue turned out to be so heavy that I would have had difficulty lifting it into my car without the help of the estate sale staff, and I had no place to store it.

*eBay* does have a provision for offering something for sale only within a local area, but that greatly restricts the market, and without knowing the name of the deity, I soon realized that I would have difficulty finding a comparable item on *eBay* and writing an informative description. As it happened, I was able to resell the statue profitably locally using *craigslist*, but I count myself very fortunate not to have been stuck with it!

## Expensive Lessons

Once in awhile I've overconfidently purchased an item in the $100 to $200 price range, certain that I knew enough about it to resell it profitably, then discovered that I had overestimated the market or that market conditions had changed for the worse. Obviously, the more you risk on an item, the more you stand to lose if you turn out to be wrong about its market appeal. Having an item fail to sell profitably is always disappointing, but taking a substantial loss on one is certainly disheartening!

# Successful Selling on *eBay* Long-term

Numerous books have been written about how to sell successfully on *eBay* and new ones appear frequently, so I'll give only the briefest of discussions of this subject here, especially since *eBay* is a continuously evolving system and its specific features change with the passage of time.

Keep in mind that in addition to all the different books available about selling on *eBay* (over 200 at the time of this writing; your local public library probably has several of them), *eBay* itself also provides detailed information online to assist with successful selling. This information includes *eBay*'s official online guides as well numerous member-contributed guides, some of which can be quite helpful. *eBay* also offers classes from time to time in major urban areas.

## Reputation and Feedback Are Key

Many people are understandably reluctant to purchase items online for various reasons, including the possibility of identity theft and the not-irrational fear of becoming the victim of a scam. One of the most important innovations of *eBay* has been to provide a way to reassure prospective buyers that they are dealing with a legitimate seller.

This method is to display a public feedback rating of each buyer and seller based on previous transactions. Each time an item is bought on *eBay*, the buyer is strongly encouraged to post a brief comment, which can be positive, negative or neutral, indicating their satisfaction or dissatisfaction with the transaction. Conversely, the seller is also encouraged to post feedback about the buyer.

This means that a prospective buyer reading an auction listing can quickly assess whether the item is offered by a reputable seller (someone with a long track record and a high positve feedback rating) or not. Sellers can also elect to reject bids by buyers who have negative feedback, for example, because they never paid for previous items they won at auction.

Since even three or four negative feedback comments about a seller will deter many prospective buyers, it's essential to avoid negative feedback to sell successfully long-term on *eBay*. The way to get positive feedback is to describe items accurately in your listings, which includes being honest about their flaws and defects, pack items carefully, and ship them within three days after receiving payment.

If for some reason (for example, because you're ill), you're unable to ship an item promptly, it's essential to e-mail the buyer to explain the delay. This will generally prevent them from leaving you negative feedback.

The prompt shipping requirement does mean that you need to plan ahead when putting items up for auction. If an item closes the day after you leave for a two-week vacation, you can definitely anticipate getting negative feedback from the buyer complaining about the delay in receiving it!

## Some Considerations in Selling Estate Sale Items

When you sell vintage collectible items on eBay, there are several things to consider, including the category in which to place it, the starting bid amount to set, the wording of the title, the amount of detail to include in the description, what methods of payment to accept, and whether to ship internationally or not, and whether to pay the fees to add features to a basic *eBay* listing.

These are discussed in detail below.

# More About Selecting Items to Buy and Resell on *eBay*

Faced with the hundreds, even thousands, of items, old and new, large and small, pristine and well-worn, offered at a typical estate sale, how can you go about selecting a few inexpensive ones likely to have a high resale value on *eBay*? As mentioned earlier, selecting items your can resell profitably is the key to successful estate sale prospecting.

A good starting point is to look for small vintage items still in their original boxes. Small items will be easiest to carry, store, pack, and ship.

An original box will give you important information about the manufacturer and the item name you can use in listing these items on *eBay*. For collectors, the box also adds to the value.

In some cases, you may be lucky enough to find an unused item still in its box. Obviously this may be a particularly valuable item. And even if the item inside is used, an original box provides evidence of its authenticity. If you know something about items of a particular nature, for example, old cameras, you can certainly draw on that knowledge to improve your success in making wise selections.

It's also helpful to know what types of items to avoid! Some examples of these have already been given earlier and others are discussed in detail below.

## General Types of Things to Avoid

In general, it's best to avoid large, bulky items, especially if they're heavy or extremely fragile, because they'll be difficult to pack and ship, not to mention to just get home in one piece! No matter how tempting that antique treadle-operated sewing machine with the polished wood cabinet may seem, it's better to let it go unless you're certain that some buyer will be willing not only to pay a reasonable price for it but to ante up for substantial shipping charges as well.

Think twice about items that have no identifying name or manufacturer, like some vases. They'll be more difficult to list on *eBay* in a way that will enable to prospective buyers to find them readily.

## Some Specific Categories of Things to Avoid

Unless you're already knowledgeable about items in the categories described below, it's best to avoid them for several reasons. First, these are types of items where it's easy to make a serious mistake during a hasty examination. Second, they're also the types of items that are immediately spotted by dealers and serious collectors, so anything that's left after the first few minutes of a well-attended estate sale will already have been picked over.

# Jewelry

People experienced in managing estate sales often put jewelry on a separate table by the door next to the cash box because they know that some buyers will be primarily interested in these items and they want to be able to keep a close eye on them because they are easily shop-lifted and some may be especially valuable. The mistakes that are easy to make with jewelry are to misjudge the antiquity of an item, as I did with the box of heart keep-sakes; to confuse a valuable type of gemstone with a less valuable one, a diamond vs. a cubic zirconium being one example; and to select something that appeals to you but not to *eBay* buyers, as I did with the straight ra-zor.

# Works of Art

Interesting as they may be, works of art are iffy because of changes in the popularity of particular artists combined with authentication issues. In addition, large prints, paintings, and statues are obviously difficult to pack and ship.

However, it you encounter an inexpensive work of art that's to your own taste, you can certainly buy it and try it on *eBay*. If it turns out that there isn't a market for it, you may still enjoy displaying on your mantelpiece or hanging it on your own wall.

# Old Books

Old books are complicated to evaluate. One important thing that affects their value is the edition and printing, which can sometimes be quite difficult to determine because different publishers use different conventions to indicate edition and printing. Signed first editions can be quite valuable, but signatures are susceptible to forgery, and the more prominent the author, the greater the incentive to forgery and the greater the necessity for authentication.

Beyond that, familiar titles often sold in large numbers, so unless they're first editions, copies are so common as to be almost valueless. Obscure books, on the other hand, may be quite rare, but most have little market.

## My Own Experience with Old Books

I consider myself moderately knowledgeable about rare and antiquarian books, but even so, my success in selecting them at estate sales has been unimpressive at best. For example, of seven old hardcover books, all in good condition, that I bought for $1 each, one sold for $6, one sold for $2, four didn't sell at all, and one I didn't even bother to list because when I checked I found that several copies had been put up for sale on *eBay* in the previous few weeks, but none had sold. Eight dollars back on a $7 investment is certainly nothing to boast about, and of course the *eBay* fees for 6 listings together with the *PayPal* fees for two transactions totaled about $1, so in the end I broke even – live and learn!

## Newer Books

I personally tend to avoid newer books (say, books published in the last 20 or 30 years), whether hardcover or paperback, on the theory that used book dealers know what there's a market for better than I do, and, while an occasional old book may fetch a high price at auction, it's very unlikely that a newer book will. Few newer books will be rare, and often used copies are readily available on *Amazon.com*, *Powells.com*, or any of a number of online used bookstores, including some *eBay* stores.

### A New Electronic Wrinkle

At a recent estate sale, I saw a fellow equipped with a handheld barcode scanner attached to a PDA or Pocket PC of some sort (maybe it was even a smart phone) rapidly going through several shelves of newer books priced at 3 for $10 for hardcovers and 3 for $5 for quality paperbacks. He'd grab a book, flip it over, scan the barcode on the back, glance at the screen, and either put the book back or set it aside to buy.

Naturally everyone was curious about what he was doing. In response to someone's question, he interrupted his scanning briefly to say that he was a used book dealer and was using the scanner to check a database (apparently an Internet one he was accessing with a wireless connection) to see if it was a book he should have for his stock. Not surprisingly, he was pretty tight-lipped about his enterprise, but he did go so far as to tell me that he didn't have a store and sold only online.

Apparently technology has created a market niche for someone who can rapidly determine the value of used books published recently enough (i.e., since 1970 or so) to have barcodes. The guess would be that the profit on each individual book is modest, but by selecting only those for which there's a market, there's money to be made for someone who's industrious and is able to pack and ship individual books efficiently.

Volume would be the key here, unlike with estate sale prospecting, where the idea is to unearth a valuable nugget here and there. I've since seen other people doing the same thing, sometimes just by keying the ISBN code on the back of a book into a cell phone, and have heard that there's a subscription service that makes it possible to check a used book's price on *Amazon.com*. Selling books online through *Amazon Marketplace* is beyond the scope of the body of this book, but is discussed briefly in the Appendix.

# Some Estate Sale Shopping Hints

Depending on where you live, you're likely to encounter any of several different general types of estate sales. Sales differ in the degree of crowding, the attention to organization, whether they are professionally managed or not, and the pricing strategy.

## Crowding

Most estate sales will have some sort of signup list or number system to admit prospective buyers in order when they first open their doors. Even so, you're likely to encounter some crowded scramble-system sales where the list or the numbers don't mean much and as many people as can possibly fit stream in through the door when it opens. These can be frustrating because it's so hard to move around and to get to things you that catch your eye before someone else snatches them up.

You may also encounter well-regulated estate sales where only a certain number of buyers are admitted at the beginning and after that people are only admitted when others leave until the crowd thins out. Once you're in the door, it's easy to move around and look at things, but waiting outside as other people leave with armloads of things has frustrations of its own.

You may also find poorly-attended estate sales where you have little competition and plenty of time to shop right from the start. Of course, most estate sales will be relatively uncrowded after the first couple of hours.

## A Shopping Basket

You may find it handy to take along a small basket, shopping bag, or cardboard box when you go to estate sales to make it easier to carry several items without damaging them. This will also make it easier to avoid putting something down so you can pick up something else to examine. Other intent shoppers may mistake whatever you've put down for something that's still available and pick it up themselves!

## Organization

You may encounter some estate sales in cramped older houses packed with items and others in newer suburban houses with relatively few items neatly laid out on tables in spacious rooms. At most estate sales, related items like glassware or Christmas ornaments will have been grouped together on tables and counters, but some hastily-arranged estate sales are very poorly organized, perhaps even with items for sale interspersed with those that are not. Good organization is characteristic of estate sales which have been planned long in advance and conducted by professional estate sale managers.

# Pricing

At most estate sales, prices will be clearly marked, even to the point of individual price tags most items, but at some sales you will need to ask the seller the price on almost everything. At some sales prices are negotiable in the extreme, with the seller just wanting to clear out a lot of stuff in a hurry. This is especially true of hastily-arranged sales conducted by out-of-town relatives.

At other sales, especially those planned long in advance and conducted by professional estate sale managers, prices will be firm, especially during the first day, and shoppers offering less will be cordially instructed to come back on the final day of the sale, when everything remaining will be half-price. Sometimes sellers will drop prices dramatically during the last hour or two on the final day of the sale. At yard sales they may start to move things to free boxes just to get rid of them.

## Selective vs. Unselective Pricing

One of the most frustrating types of estate sales to encounter is one with unselective pricing. This is a pricing strategy in which the holder of the sale simply prices all items high and leaves it to buyers to sort through and identify those few that are worth the price.

An example would be a sale at which hundreds of old hardcover books are indiscriminately priced at $5 each. Only experienced dealers will have any idea which might be worth anything approaching that – there's not much incentive to take a chance on something here!

More interesting from a prospecting standpoint are sales with selective pricing, where many items are priced low and only those that are recognized as collectibles carry steep price tags.

# What to Expect When You First Start Out

When you first start out, don't expect to make a lot of money on your first few purchases. Estate sale prospecting, even taking full advantage of *craigslist* and *eBay*, is definitely not a get-rich-quick proposition!

Instead, expect to make plenty of mistakes. If you're lucky, one out of five of the first few dozen items you buy will turn out to do well for you on *eBay*. The other four will be mistakes of one sort or another, including items that don't sell at all, ones that sell at a loss, and ones that sell at only a minuscule profit. Hopefully the one item of five that does well will do well enough to more than compensate for the four mistakes.

If you're new to selling on *eBay*, you'll probably find you make some mistakes in setting up your first few listings too. Fortunately most of these are easily corrected if they're caught before any bids are placed on an item. You'll probably also make the occasional mistake of underestimating shipping costs, especially if you elect to sell to international buyers.

Another thing you can expect to experience, especially when you first start out, is periods of discouragement. It may help to keep in mind the game of baseball, which has some things in common with estate sale prospecting, as discussed in a later section.

## Where Does All The Time Go?

If you're not already familiar with selling items on *eBay*, you'll probably find that estate sale prospecting takes a lot more time than you'd think at first. Each step of the process takes time – finding estate sales, traveling to them, shopping at them, photographing items, weighing and measuring them, researching them, writing descriptions of them, setting starting bids, creating the listings, answering questions from potential bidders, packing items, shipping them, and leaving feedback.

## The Limits to Efficiency

It goes without saying that being well-organized and efficient will reduce the time required to sell items on *eBay*. It helps to have a staging area where you can sort out new purchases, a storage area for packing materials, and so forth.

If you were operating a home-based cottage industry like selling your own line of machine-stitched embroidered potholders online, you could improve efficiency by having standard photographs, standard item descriptions, and predetermined shipping weights. However, the nature of estate sale prospecting is that you're likely to end up with an assortment of one-of-a-kind items that will need to be individually photographed and described.

You can save some time by photographing a series of items in a single photo session, but aside from this you're likely to find it difficult to think of ways to really speed up the process. The best you may be able to do is to combine these activities with something like watching your favorite television program so the time involved passes pleasantly.

## Where The Time Gets Even Longer

It would be tempting to say "It takes just as long to sell a cheap item as an expensive one," but this turns out not to be strictly true. For example, you're likely to find that you spend more time and take more care to wrap and pack a glass vase that sold for $50 than one that sold for $5.

More importantly, the higher the value at auction of a vintage collectible item, the more e-mail questions you're likely to receive from prospective *eBay* buyers prudently seeking to confirm their condition or authenticity. These may include requests for additional photographs and for exact measurements.

# A Sports Analogy: Baseball

Estate sale prospecting can be fun, but, to repeat what I've said several times already, it certainly can't be characterized as an easy way to make money! A sports analogy drawn from baseball may be helpful at this point; after all, nobody says playing Major League baseball is an easy route to riches either!

In estate sale prospecting, you buy items you think you'll be able resell at a profit on *eBay* and then find out if you were right or not. Like baseball games, *eBay* auctions unfold at a slow pace and, just as a batter often strikes out, you'll often misjudge the value of an item at auction. If you're lucky, you may hit an occasional grand slam home run, but, like most Major League baseball players, to the extent that you succeed, it will probably be through unglamorous base hits.

## The Glacial Pace of *eBay* Auctions

The first analogy to baseball is, of course, that like baseball games, *eBay* auctions move slowly much of the time. Going to an estate sale and watching the ending of an item at auction may hold some excitement, but things can move very slowly during the week between the posting of an auction listing and its closing.

## Your Batting Average

Your batting average in estate sale prospecting is, of course, your success in picking items you can resell at a profit. Whether it's a large profit or a small one comes under "Base Hits vs. Grand Slams" below.

A sale at a loss is like a ground out in baseball – disappointing, but at least something happened. As the sportscasters are fond of observing, at least the ball was put in play. Most disappointing of all is an item that draws no bids – you struck out completely on that one!

The key point here is not to expect to bat a thousand (a batting average of 1.000, or a hit very at-bat) by having every item you select sell at a profit. Batting five hundred (0.500, or one hit in every two at-bats), even for a short period, is a remarkable achievement for a Major League hitter, and even the best hitters strike out often.

Batting three hundred (0.300) is quite respectable, and will certainly include a lot of strikeouts. As a rookie at estate sale prospecting, don't be too surprised if you find that you're batting a hundred (0.200, or one profitable item out of 5) to begin with, with lots of strikeouts.

## Base Hits vs. Grand Slams

The most exciting event in baseball is the grand slam home run, the one that scores four runs because the bases are already loaded. However, grand slam home runs are rare. Even the best batters seldom hit more than 3 or 4 over a 150-game season. Base hits are much more common and far less glamorous, but a series of them can add up to several home runs too.

The remarkable finds featured on *Antique Road Show* are grand slam home runs. You'll be very fortunate indeed if you can achieve one. Mostly when you succeed at estate sale prospecting, it will be with base hits – items resold for a pleasing profit, but not an astronomical one.

## Ground Outs

Ground outs, in which your item sells, but at a loss, are nonetheless encouraging in that they indicate you succeeded in the basic task of picking an item for which there's a market, and you have the consolation that at least you get some of your money back.

They're discouraging too, though, because they didn't achieve the goal of picking profitable items to resell.

Just as discouragement is part of the game of baseball, it's part of estate sale prospecting!

However, if you've stuck to buying inexpensive items, at least you won't have lost much money when you have a ground out.

## Striking Out

Strikeouts, items that don't sell at all, factor into your batting average too. Like ground outs, they're discouraging, and you'll probably find that you make all too many of them, especially at first. Again, if you've stuck with picking inexpensive items to buy, the depths of your discouragement will be lessened.

## Improving Your Batting Average

Professional baseball players are constantly working on improving their batting averages. As frequently observed in the sports press, they go through streaks and slumps, moments of exhilaration and periods of discouragement. Regardless of how well they're doing, they're constantly focused on improving.

In estate sale prospecting, you'll find that there are many lessons to learn about which types of items you encounter will actually find a market on *eBay* and which will not. The goal isn't to bat a thousand and hit nothing but grand slams, since that would be as unrealistic in estate sale prospecting as it is in baseball, but to operate either profitably if you are pursuing estate sale prospecting as a business, or enjoyably if you are doing it as a hobby.

A secondary goal is to improve as you gain experience. By patiently buying a few items at a time, putting them up for auction, and seeing how well they do, you'll gradually develop an eye for items with definite resale value. This will take time because you'll seldom encounter a valuable item at an estate sale exactly like one you've successfully sold already. You may also find it interesting and helpful to study books and online information on antiques and collectibles in preparation for going to estate sales. Several books on selling on *eBay* touch on this topic and at least one covers it in depth.

## Streaks and Slumps

Streaks and slumps are worth expanding on a little, since you're sure to encounter them, and an extended slump can be very disheartening. You may experience periods where item after item fails to draw a single bid on *eBay*.

When first you post some new listings and check the next day to see how they're doing, it will be with a feeling of anticipation. If, as the days go by, not a single one of them draws a bid, your anticipation will turn to discouragement. Again, keep in mind here that, although achieving a consistently high level of performance is unquestionably the goal of every professional baseball player, even league-leading hitters go through slumps, sometimes lengthy ones.

### What to Do with Items that Don't Sell?

In some cases you may want to lower the starting bid and relist an item that didn't sell at auction just to try to clear it out and get a little money out of it, especially since *eBay* will refund the second listing fee if your item sells the second time around. You'll probably find that some relisted items still don't sell, and for other items you may decide there isn't much point in relisting them.

One thing to do with items that don't sell on *eBay* is set them aside to put in your own garage or yard sale at some future date! You're not likely to get an especially good price for any of them, but you'll probably find that certain items sell better to someone who can physically examine them than they do via a photograph.

The market at garage and yard sales is different, too. People who shop these sales will be looking for anything that might be interesting or useful. They'll sometimes buy on impulse, whereas *eBay* buyers can take their time and will usually be looking for a specific item or for items within a specific category. And, of course, unlike with *eBay* items, there's no shipping charge on garage or yard sale items.

Things that don't sell at a garage or yard sale can be donated to charity.

# Assessing Your Return on Investment

Accounting isn't an enthralling activity for most people, and if you're interested in estate sale prospecting strictly as a hobby, it may not be a particularly important one. However, if you're pursuing estate sale prospecting as a business, careful ongoing bookkeeping and accounting are essential. Fortunately, much of the necessary bookkeeping is handled automatically by *eBay* and *PayPal*.

Without going into the business aspects in any depth here because there are already a number of books on operating an *eBay* business, the key thing is to be able to calculate your return on investment. This requires keeping accurate records of how much you've spent to acquire and resell items, including gasoline, shipping materials, postage, and *eBay* and *PayPal* fees, as well as how much those items eventually sold for.

## Calculating Return on Investment

As previously discussed, you'll likely find that many items you put up for auction don't sell at all, others sell for about what you paid for them, and, if you're lucky, a few sell for far more than you would have guessed. In the baseball analogy drawn above, you have a low batting average and mainly base hits.

A simple measure of your return on investment is the amount you get back for every dollar invested, after taking into account incidental expenses like gasoline as well as the direct expenses of purchasing items for re-sale, listing fees, and shipping costs. One of the attractive aspects of estate sale prospecting is the possibility of obtaining a large return on a small investment – the $1 item that turns out to bring $50 at auction, for example.

To calculate overall return on investment, you need to add up all the expenses involved with buying a series of items and reselling them, including expenses for any items that didn't sell, and subtract this amount from the total sales figure. If you put 10 items up for auction at a total cost of $17, including all non-postage expenses, and they brought in $55, including $5 in actual postage expenses prepaid by the buyers, your return on investment is $33, or a little better than $2 for every dollar you spent. Notice that postage expenses paid in advance by the buyers are treated differently here because they are prepaid rather than out-of-pocket, so they can't properly be considered an investment.

## A Simple Example

As a very simple example, imagine that you bought 10 items at estate sales for $1 each. Imagine also that the sales were quite nearby and close together, so your gasoline expenses were only $1. You set the starting bids at $0.99, so the *eBay* listing fees for these 10 items totaled only $2. Of these, only one item sold, but it went for $50 and the buyer prepaid $5 for the postage. Suppose that the *eBay* final value fee for this item was $2 and the buyer paid $55 with *PayPal*, so there was also a *PayPal* fee of $2. You recycled an old box to ship this item, so there was no cost for shipping materials. This is one scenario in which you could get a return of $33 on a $15 investment, or a little better than $2 on the $1.

## Improving Your Batting Average

In the simple example above, your batting average was only a hundred (0.100, 1 item out of 10 sold), but you did get a pretty good hit, one that might qualify as a triple in baseball terminology. If you can improve your ability to pick inexpensive items that will sell, even if it's only for $5 or $10 apiece, your return on investment will go up. Obviously it would be wonderful to be able to pick items that will resell for profits that qualify as home runs, but learning what items there will be no market for, so you won't buy more of them in the future, helps improve your overall batting average and thus contributes to your future return on investment.

# Some Concluding Advice

If you're just getting started in estate sale prospecting, and especially if you're new at selling on *eBay*, here are some things to keep in mind.

## Test the Waters

Because many factors can affect your success in estate sale prospecting (your geographic location being a key one, for example), it's prudent to test the waters by making the absolute minimum investment necessary to get started and by starting slowly. Plan to go through at least one full cycle of finding estate sales, buying a few inexpensive items, photographing them, listing them on *eBay*, receiving payment, packing and shipping those that sell, and getting buyer feedback before committing to estate sale prospecting as an ongoing activity. This first cycle will probably take at least 10 days.

If you find that the time commitment and frustrations outweigh the rewards, you've lost little. If you find you do enjoy estate sale prospecting and conclude that it's a promising endeavor, you're now set to forge ahead and work on improving your success.

### The Quickest Test

As mentioned earlier, the quickest way to test the

waters is to try taking a few items you think will sell for $30 or more each to an "I Sold It On *eBay*" store if there's one near you.

## Start Small

Don't go overboard rushing from one estate sale to another and buying armloads of items at the outset. Remember that each individual item will take considerable time to photograph, research, describe, weigh, list on *eBay*, and pack and ship if it sells. You may also need to answer answer e-mail questions from prospective buyers.

Especially when you're first starting out, you're likely to find that a high percentage of the items you buy don't have the market you hoped they would on *eBay*, so you'll end up taking a loss on them. And if items do sell on *eBay*, you don't want to fall behind in shipping them because that will lead to unhappy buyers concerned that they have been scammed, possible negative feedback, and perhaps even suspension as an *eBay* seller!

If you're just doing estate sale prospecting as a hobby, you'll want not just to start small but to stay small.

## Set a Buying Budget and Stick to It

Decide in advance how much money you're comfortable risking to buy items that, no matter how enticing they may seem at an estate sale, may not turn out to have any market at all. And don't let yourself be stampeded into spending more than you've budgeted just because others around you are exuberantly carting off armloads of things from a sale!

## Buy Cheap

Unless you're *absolutely* sure what you are buying, don't spend more than, say, $10 on a single item – an amount you won't feel bad about writing off as a loss if that item turns out not to sell on *eBay*. Buying several cheap items instead of a single more expensive one is one way of hedging your estate sale prospecting bets.

## One Thing at a Time

At estate sales you'll sometimes encounter large quantities of some type of item that seems to have potential. When you're just starting out, only buy one or two, not dozens!

This is true even if you see others buying up quantities of something or other! You'll miss some great opportunities by doing this, but you'll also avoid gambling a large sum of money and losing it all.

### An Example – Avon Collectibles

At one estate sale I went to, a side room in the basement had hundreds of Avon items, some of them still in their original boxes, for $2 each. Several people were looking through them and one man, evidently a dealer, was filling a shopping bag with boxed items he carefully selected one by one.

Were there some valuable pieces there? Certainly, as the interest of the dealer indicated, but probably most of the Avon items had little or no market. If I'd impulsively bought 50 items I knew absolutely nothing about just because I had the opportunity to do so, I suspect I'd have been lucky to get 10 cents on the dollar on my hundred-dollar investment!

## There's Always Another Estate Sale . . .

Especially if you live in an urban area, if you miss out on buying an item you want because someone else snaps it up first while you debate with yourself about it, remind yourself, "There's always another estate sale." The nature of estate sales is that what you'll find at the next one is completely unpredictable, and there may well be something far more valuable at auction than whatever you just missed out on.

This is especially true because you're only after a few items. Generally speaking, no one item is certain to have an enormous impact on your long-term results.

### What If There's An Estate Sale Drought?

What if you hit a period when there are simply not any estate sales within a reasonable distance, especially if it's also the wrong weather or season for garage sales, yard sales, and rummage sales? You might try dropping by your local thrift store.

If you do, when you starting look at price tags you'll probably rapidly conclude that the store's staff is tuned in to what may be a collectible and has set prices optimistically, perhaps even over-optimistically. You'll probably also notice people you suspect are dealers picking over the merchandise and snapping up selected books as well as certain types of collectibles. Nonetheless, there's probably an occasional obscure vintage collectible item that slips through unrecognized and is priced reasonably enough that you can make a profit reselling it on *eBay* if you spot it.

## Start with Basic *eBay* Listings

To keep costs to a minimum and gain experience with selling on *eBay*, start with the most basic possible listings. This means only one category, an item title but no subtitle, just one photograph, no gallery option (making a well-worded title especially important!), no reserve amount, and no special added features. Later on you can start to try adding more photos and other special auction features to see if they really make a difference in selling vintage collectible items or not.

Accept only *PayPal* payments and do not ship internationally. This will keep things as simple as possible to start with, and you won't have to worry about bounced checks, customs declaration forms, and Nigerian scams.

Ship mainly by U.S. Postal Service Priority Mail and *always* use delivery confirmation (free for Priority Mail if you can weigh your packages accurately and print your own shipping labels with *PayPal*). Signature confirmation will not usually be necessary; delivery confirmation will suffice if a dispute arises over whether a buyer received an item or not.

The goal in all this is to start building up a history of smooth transactions resulting in good feedback from satisfied buyers. Especially in your early transactions, go to great lengths to keep buyers happy, even if you loose money on the transaction as a result. One negative feedback comment in your first four transactions will give you only a 75% positive feedback rating – very low by *eBay* standards!

As you progress, you can begin to experiment judiciously with other payment and shipping methods and with shipping internationally to gain access to the global market for your items.

# A Global Online Market for the Most Surprising Things!

Without question, *eBay* has created a global electronic marketplace in which the most surprising things turn out to have significant value! This creates a genuine opportunity for estate sale prospecting as an income-producing activity.

The beauty of *eBay* is that it makes it relatively easy and inexpensive to determine the market for even obscure items, either by reviewing items presently up for auction or recently sold or by putting them up for bid. Although few items found at a typical estate sale will bring a substantial profit, many may bring some return on your initial investment.

## Why No Competition from Companies?

When profitable business opportunities emerge, alert companies expand into them. If estate sale prospecting really works, why aren't there companies that specialize in doing it?

Certainly a company could hire people and send them to estate sales to seek out undervalued items and bring them back to a central office, where other staff members would photograph them and list them for sale on *eBay*. However, it would be difficult to monitor these employees, who would have to be entrusted with large amounts of cash, and they would probably be paid at the low end of the wage scale, so many would find themselves tempted to supplement their income by purchasing plum items out of their own pockets and reselling them on the side.

Certainly owners of antique stores and used bookstores frequent estate sales and bring their finds back to their stores, where they may have staff to handle the listing and sales, but the buying is not typically something they delegate because their years of acquired personal expertise add so much value for this function. For this reason, estate sale prospecting is likely always to remain the province of the small independent buyer, not an army of professional shoppers employed by a company.

Of course, for particularly valuable estates, especially those with art collections, the auction houses do fulfill this function and will send people to appraise items and handle their sale.

## But Is It for You?

Granting that estate sale prospecting using *craigslist* and *eBay* can indeed be a profitable hobby or a home-based small business, is it for you? This is a question only you can answer. The factors you need to take into account in making a decision include your geographic location, your degree of comfort with computer technology, including digital cameras and online auctions, and your other time commitments.

Fortunately estate sale prospecting is an endeavor for which you can test the waters without making a large initial investment and find out if, in your particular situation, the rewards outweigh the effort and frustrations.

# Acknowledgments

I thank my former spouse Nancy Coomer for encouraging me to pursue estate sale prospecting and for drawing my attention at estate and yard sales to items of particular interest from time to time.

# Appendix: *Amazon Marketplace*

## Online Sales of Used Books

*Amazon Marketplace* is perhaps the primary place used by people who buy newer books at yard sales to sell them online. It operates on a different model than *eBay* auctions. Of course, *Amazon.com* has its own auctions, but *Amazon Marketplace* has some unique advantages, the biggest being a high level of visibility for listings because search results for a specific book include used copies as well as new ones.

*Amazon Marketplace* is tailored for selling individual books, as opposed to sets or lots, and saves time by automatically filling in the basic item description. All that needs be done to create a listing is to search for a book by title, author, or ISBN, click the "Sell One Like This" button, set the price and add a descriptive comment such as "Good condition, cover somewhat scuffed." There's no cost at all if a book doesn't sell within 60 days, after which the listing expires.

However, the cost if a book does sell is nontrivial-a $0.99 per book transaction fee, plus a closing fee that is set at $1.20 per book, and on top of that a 15% commission based on the selling price. The standard shipping and handling cost to the buyer for a book is $3.99.

Thus a $10 book would cost the buyer $13.99 plus tax. The seller would get $13.99 less the $0.99 transaction fee, the $1.20 closing fee, and the $1.50 commission (total $3.69), or a payment of $11.31. If the book can be shipped for $2, the seller would be receiving $1.99 for handling, yielding a total of $9.31 after the order is filled. They would receive their payment of $11.31 from Amazon Payments deposited directly to their bank account within two weeks, but would be required to ship the book within a day or two after the purchase is made, as explained in the next section.

Unlike *PayPal*, *Amazon.com* apparently doesn't provide a way for sellers to purchase postage and print out shipping labels. However, it does have helpful discussion boards that allow *Amazon Marketplace* sellers to share tips, ideas, and experiences.

## Seller Requirements

Unlike *eBay* auctions, where the seller has great latitude in writing the item description and can set the shipping costs and the handling time, *Amazon Marketplace* imposes certain requirements on sellers of books. The standard shipping cost for a book is $3.99, and orders are required to be filled within two business days. This is mandated even though Amazon only disburses accumulated payments (less transaction fees, closing fees, and commissions) every two weeks by direct deposit to the seller's bank account. Item description comments concerning condition must conform to a list of standard definitions.

## The Pro Merchant Seller Account

The $0.99 per-item transaction fee can be eliminated by becoming a Pro Merchant seller and paying a $19.99 per month introductory fee for the first two months, increasing to $39.99 per month thereafter. Obviously becoming a Pro Merchant seller makes economic sense for people selling more than 20 to 40 books a month.

A Pro Merchant seller account also means that listings never expire, which has the advantage of creating a personal online store linked directly into *Amazon.com*'s high-traffic search engine. This is presumably how most people who prospect for used books using a cell phone or PDA (or maybe "assay" is more appropriate than "prospect" here) sell their wares, and rumor has it that there's a subscription service that tells how much used books are currently worth on *Amazon.com* which includes a downloadable ISBN database for Pocket PC's. Of course, Google's Froogle service can also find used book prices based on ISBN and do it for free, but it's not clear that its queries search *Amazon Marketplace*.

One catch with *Amazon Marketplace* is that you can see how used books are priced there, but you can't tell how rapidly they sell. Unlike with *eBay*, there's no way to view completed listings, nor if a listing ends, is there a way to determine whether the book sold or if the listing simply expired.

# Book Pricing in *Amazon Marketplace*

I personally find that books by my favorite authors (who include P. D. James, Tony Hillerman, John Le-Carre, and Ngaio Marsh) catch my eye at yard and rummage sales. However, the law of supply and demand enters in here in determining their value.

British mystery writer P. D. James has very popular for decades, so hundreds of used copies of her books are listed in *Amazon Marketplace*, dozens of them with prices as low as $0.01. A copy selling for $0.01 would cost the customer $4 with the standard $3.99 charge for shipping and handling, of which $1.20 to $2.19 would go for Amazon fees, depending on the type of seller account, leaving nothing after postage for a casual seller or $0.42 for a Pro Merchant seller (neglecting acquisition costs and shipping materials).

Interestingly, hardcover editions as well as mass market paperbacks are listed for as little as $0.01 to $0.48 in *Amazon Marketplace*. The low end of the pricing scale is in this range for Tony Hillerman mysteries as well as for the more popular of John LeCarre's spy novels. Pricing is higher for some of LeCarre's more obscure books, but it's hard to know in advance how much of a market there actually is for them.

## When a Penny Book is Really a $4 Book

Because of the standard $3.99 shipping and handling charge, a book priced at $0.01 in *Amazon Marketplace* is really a $4 book from the buyer's standpoint. For this reason, a popular (and therefore common) fiction book may sell readily for $0.50 or $1 at a garage or yard sale when it wouldn't sell at all at that price in *Amazon Marketplace* because of the price competition from all the $0.01 copies.

## Conclusions

The first assessment of *Amazon Marketplace* for common used books typically encountered at estate sales would be "a lot of work for very little money." However, it might be possible for an estate sale prospector to learn to recognize a few high-value books that would be profitable to pick up for $1 or less at yard sales. These would likely include unread copies of out-of-print nonfiction hardcover books that initially carried a high price tag.

.

CPSIA information can be obtained at www.ICGtesting.com
Printed in the USA
LVOW062350131211

259227LV00001B/105/A